A Widow's Cry

A helpful tool for widow ministries

Jamie Pulos-Fry

James 1:27

ReadersMagnet, LLC

A Widow's Cry
Copyright © 2023 by Jamie Pulos-Fry

Published in the United States of America

Library of Congress Control Number: 2024904529
ISBN   Paperback: 979-8-89091-502-3
ISBN   eBook: 979-8-89091-503-0

All rights reserved. No part of this publication may be reproduced, stored in a retrieval system or transmitted in any way by any means, electronic, mechanical, photocopy, recording or otherwise without the prior permission of the author except as provided by USA copyright law.

The opinions expressed by the author are not necessarily those of ReadersMagnet, LLC.

ReadersMagnet, LLC
10620 Treena Street, Suite 230 | San Diego, California, 92131 USA
1.619. 354. 2643 | www.readersmagnet.com

Book design copyright © 2023 by ReadersMagnet, LLC. All rights reserved.
First Published in 2020.
Interior design by Karin Whitler and Dorothy Lee

"Jamie has put a lot of heart and soul into this book.... For she has lived it! It is chock-full of information and resources.

There are now things I will never say to a widow—thank you!"

—Mrs. Tonya Shepherd, Woman's Inspirational Speaker

"Very helpful book! Very challenging to do more, pray more, and invest more in widows."

—Mrs. Suza Rasmussen, instructor, West Coast Baptist College, Lancaster, California

DEDICATION

This book is dedicated to a special friend, Nancy Lusk,

First, for being my friend before she was even a widow herself, then for encouraging me to write my first two books and for being the reason for writing this one;

Second, for reminding me that widows are important and are still needed in this world. I have been a widow for over 24 years and wonder sometimes why God still needs me; Third, by using a few of her many gifts: for singing in the music ministry at our church beside me every Sunday, for working with the children's ministry as school teacher and helper, plus volunteering for Vacation Bible School and for serving meals for the college students at West Coast Baptist College.

TABLE OF CONTENTS

Foreword 6
Acknowledgments 7
Introduction 8

Chapter One - Prayer 11
Chapter Two - Visits...20
Chapter Three - Phone Calls.....................................23
Chapter Four - Grief Counseling 32
Chapter Five - Widows Support Groups....................38
Chapter Six - Encouraging Books To Read 44
Chapter Seven - Websites To Checkout 51
Chapter Eight - Financial Help..................................55
Chapter Nine - Church Help.....................................60

Conclusion 65
Index of Scriptures 70
Reference Books..72
About the Author..73

FOREWORD

This book came to be because my mother of 80 years said, "Did you ever think that you would be a writer?" The answer to that was "No." I had a hard time with English growing up and had to work extra hard to get my writing up to par.

Then I prayed to God what He would have me write this time. That small voice from God said that it has to be something that I am or that I do. Well, I am a widow and widows always need guidance.

So, I started doing some research, and this book is the result of that research from a faithful widow.

ACKNOWLEDGMENTS

I am thankful to many people for their generous contributions to make this book possible.

First, I'm thankful for all the widows out there who serve alongside me every week at church and my daily life.

Second, I wish to thank those godly widows who have been my good examples throughout the different stages of my life. Many are still encouraging me through their consistent godliness: Mrs. Ellen Pulos, Mrs. Winifred Brunston, Mrs. Nancy Lusk, Mrs. Jo Ann Eaton, and so many others.

Third, I would like to thank those who helped with the proofreading, designing, and publishing of this book. It would not have come to be without all their hard work. Thank you.

Fourth, I would like to thank the Lord for making me a widow so early in my life, so I could share this information with the world with a kind and giving heart.

Thank you. Amen.

INTRODUCTION

Do widows matter? Yes, they do matter. And although you may not understand or are afraid of widows, there are four benefits that you will receive or learn from helping a widow.

1) **There are around about 27 verses in the Bible that tell us they matter.** *The Bible is a great resource for teaching us to understand and not to be afraid of widows.*

2) **A widow will understand about prayer in time, because they end up being prayer warriors in the future.** *By helping a widow, you are giving her your time. By giving freely of your time, you know that you are making a positive difference in the lives of others.*

3) **Visiting a widow is great because when we give them the honor they deserve, we find out that we can learn so many things from them.** *When you spend time helping a widow, you actually draw closer to God. You feel more connected to Jesus and His teachings and the way of life that He practiced and advocated. The more you read this book the more it will show you the many reasons that Jesus taught that widows matter.*

4) A widow will be a great servant if she maintains her joy of life through committed personal ministry readiness to "be there" and lovingly helps address the speed bumps or barriers along the way. *When you visit or make phone calls to widows, you are not only enriching their lives, but you also grow personally, spiritually, and socially. You learn more about the widows and their ways and you also develop self-confidence and self-esteem, characteristics that help you no matter where you are.*

Helping a widow is a great honor for many reasons: one being a helper or volunteer strictly for the practice of unselfish concern for the welfare of that widow. Another would be going out of your way to aid a stranger. A third reason would be just to help someone without expecting anything in return but a smile.

A Widow Helper or Church Widow Volunteer Definition:

Ministry helpers or church widow volunteers include pastors, staff, teachers with their students if the church has a school, deacons and their wives, and numerous other adults with children, both singles and couples, college students with a car if the church has a college, all with a heart to minister to these special ladies who have so much to give.

Please look at some of the ideas that I have put in this book about making you a better ministry helper or church widow volunteer.

I hope they help you to be the best ministry helper or church widow volunteer you can be and care for others from your heart.

CHAPTER ONE

"Honor widows that are widows indeed."
(Timothy 5:3)

Prayer

How to grieve in a healthy way by using

John 11:32-37:

32 Then when Mary was come where Jesus was, and saw him, she fell down at his feet, saying unto him, "Lord, if thou hadst been here, my brother would not have died."

33 When Jesus therefore saw her weeping, and the Jews also weeping which came with her, he groaned in the spirit, and was troubled,

34 And said, "Where have ye laid him?" They said unto him, "Lord, come and see."

35 Jesus wept.

36 Then said the Jews, "Behold how he loved him!"

37 And some of them said, "Could not this man, which opened the eyes of the blind, have caused that even this man should not have died?"

When supporting those grieving:

1. Serving a hurting heart is sowing seeds that bring a great harvest. Have you served someone this week? Go visit a widow this week. "Bear ye one another's burdens, and so fulfil the law of Christ." (Galatians 6:2)
2. Offer up support; don't press it if unaccepted. It may not be the right time, and not everyone is welcome in the innermost place of grief. Put aside your wants and pray over your role.
3. Pray: Prayer is a powerful tool and privilege, not a last resort. It's the best way to get started in approaching the person. Never make light of prayer.

4. There are phrases that do not help. In fact, they are both hurtful and damaging to someone already in pain. Here are a few:

"God never gives you more than you can handle," "I know how you feel," and "It's just God's plan."

The most honest offering I have ever heard is: "I really don't know what to say, but I want you to know that I care."

5. Tears are very important in the healthy grieving process. Never tell someone not to cry. I always tell them that when my husband passed, that after his service, when I was home and alone, I cried for hours. Never be ashamed of your own tears. Jesus wept, too. Tears are not a sign of weakness; they are a gift to help us grieve. Without them, healing cannot and will not come.

When we pray for others, we are helping them gain strength to get through the day. Prayer is influential to our lives and others' lives. When we are praying, God is working.

Here are a few verses about prayer — God showing us that we need to pray for widows: "I exhort therefore, that, first of all, supplications, prayers, intercessions, and giving of thanks, be made for all men; 2 For kings, and for all that are in authority; that we may lead a quiet and peaceable life in all godliness and honesty. 3 For this is good and acceptable in the sight of God our Saviour;

4 Who will have all men to be saved, and to come unto the knowledge of the truth." (I Timothy 2:1-4)

Widows Honor Chapter:

1   Rebuke not an elder, but treat *him* as a father; *and* the younger men as brethren;
2   The elder women as mothers; the younger as sisters, with all purity.
3   Honor widows who are widows indeed.
4   But if any widow has children or nephews, let them learn first to shew piety at home, and to requite their parents: for that is good and acceptable before God.
5   Now she who is a widow indeed, and desolate, trusteth in God, and continueth in supplications and prayers night and day.
6   But she that liveth in pleasure is dead while she liveth.
7   And these things give in charge, that they may be blameless.
8   But if any provide not for his own, and especially for those of his own house, he hath denied the faith, and is worse than an infidel.
9   Let not a widow be taken into the number under threescore years old, having been the wife of one man,
10 Well reported of for good works; if she has brought up children, if she has lodged strangers, if she has washed the saints' feet, if she has relieved the afflicted, if she has diligently followed every good work.

11 But the younger widows refuse: for when they have begun to wax wanton against Christ, they will marry;

12 Having damnation, because they have cast off their first faith.

13 And withal they learn *to be* idle, wandering about from house to house; and not only idle, but tattlers also and busybodies, speaking things which they ought not.

14 I will therefore that the younger women marry, bear children, guide the house, give none occasion to the adversary to speak reproachfully.

15 For some are already turned aside after Satan.

16 If any man or woman who believeth have widows, let them relieve them, and let not the church be charged; that it may relieve them that are widows indeed.

17 Let the elders who rule well be counted worthy of double honor, especially they who labor in the word and doctrine. (1 Timothy 5: 1-17)

Here is a prayer that will help you to pray for widows.

"Thank you, Father, for bringing this widow into my life and giving me a chance to help her with this prayer. I commit myself to pray and not to turn coward —- faint, lose heart, or give up.

Fearlessly and confidently and boldly, I draw near to the throne of grace that I may receive mercy and find grace to help in times of need for every need — coming just when I (and others) need it.

When I do not know what prayer to offer and how to offer it worthily as I ought, I thank You, Father, that the Holy Spirit comes to my aid and bears me up in my weakness.

I do not fear or have any anxiety about anything, but that in every circumstance and in everything by prayer and petition (definite requests), with thanksgiving continue to make my needs (and the needs of others) known to God. Whatever I ask for in prayer, I believe that it will be granted to me, and I will receive it.

The earnest heartfelt prayer of a righteous man makes tremendous power available. Father, I live in You — abide united to you — and Your words remain in me and live in my heart. Therefore, I will ask and it shall be done for me. When I bear (produce) much fruit (through prayer), You, Father, are honored and glorified in it. Amen!"

God can help you with your fears and worries:

Something to think about when planning and problems are pre-occupying your mind, turn to Him and whisper His Name. Let the Light of His Presence shine on you as you rejoice in His unfailing Love.

Thank Him for watching over you and loving you eternally. Affirm your trust in Him; express your devotion to Him. Then ask Him to illuminate the way forward — helping you sort out what needs to be done today and what does not. Deal with problems as you must, but refuse to let worry or fear become central in your thoughts.

Keep returning your focus to Him as often as you can, and He will light up your perspective.

Saturate your mind and heart with Scripture —-reading it, studying it, and memorizing verses that are especially helpful to you. *Thy word is* a *lamp unto my feet, and* a *light unto my path* (Psalm 119:105).

If you follow these guidelines, your preoccupation with planning and problems will diminish. This leaves room in your life for more of Him. Delight in *the Joy of His Presence!*

Here is something to change your Biblical behavior about anxiety by breaking down the word FEAR in the Bible:

F — Faith in God's Word (Luke 8:22-25)
E — Exam the Fear (Is it real?) (Joshua 1:9)
A — Attack it head on (Daniel 3:16-18)
R — Request God's help (Philippians 4:6)

This has helped me to release the painful uneasiness of the mind about future things and about controlling things in my life.

Here are a few prayers that you may want to read to widows who are having problems with fear and worry:

VICTORY OVER FEAR

Father, in Jesus' name, I confess and believe that no weapon formed against me shall prosper, and any tongue that rises against me in judgment I shall show to be in the wrong. I believe I dwell in the secret place of the Most High. I believe the wisdom of God's Word dwells in me, and because of that, I am without fear or dread of evil. He directs and makes straight my path.

I am strengthened and reinforced with Holy Spirit's mighty power that dwells in me. God is my strength and my refuge, and I trust in Him and in His Word. I am empowered through my fellowship with Almighty God.

God Himself has said, "Let your conversation be without covetousness; and be content with such things as ye have: for he hath said, I will never leave thee, nor forsake thee." (Hebrews 13:5)

I take comfort and am encouraged, and confidently and boldly, "The Lord is my helper. I will not fear or be terrified, for what can man do to me?"

I confess and believe that my children are disciples taught of the Lord and obedient to God's will. God will perfect that which concerns me and

He gives my children safety and eases them through this time.

This is the Word of God, alive and full of power, it energizes me, and it affects me. As I speak God's Word, it is healing to my flesh. It is prosperity to me. According to His Word that I have spoken, so be it, in Jesus' name! Amen.

TO LIVE FREE FROM WORRY

Father, I thank You that I have been delivered from the power of darkness and translated into the Kingdom of your dear Son. I commit to live free from worry in the name of Jesus, for the law of the Spirit of life in Christ Jesus has made me free from the law of sin and death.

I humble myself under Your mighty hand that in your time, You may exalt me. I cast the whole of my cares (name them) —- all my anxieties, all my worries, all my concerns —- on You. You will sustain me and will never allow me to slip, fall, or fail!

I cast down imaginations (reasonings) and every high thing that exalts itself against the knowledge of You. I lay aside every weight and the sin of worry which does try to beset me. I run with patience the race that is set before me, looking unto Jesus, the author and finisher of my faith.

Thank You, Father, for making me carefree that I can walk in that peace which passes all understanding, in Jesus' Christ name! Amen.

CHAPTER TWO

"Pure religion and undefiled before God and the Father is this: to visit the fatherless and widows in their affliction, and to keep himself unspotted from the world."

(James 1:27)

Visits

When you go to visit a widow, always pray before you go (and with your partner).

Prayer for Widows

— Vienna Cobb Anderson

Most loving God, you know the pain and sorrow of death; mercifully hear our prayer for those who mourn the death of their beloved. The nights are lonely and the days are too long. Comfort them and bring an end to the days of tears. Bless them and bring an end to their days of sorrow. Renew them with the joy of life and bring to an end their days of mourning. Let the bond of love which you have for your people be the foundation of their hope that love never ends and that precious moments with our beloved are forever held dear in our hearts. Amen.

Read more at http://www.beliefnet.com/prayers/multifaith/death/prayer-for-widows.aspx#dhm33I1hQWskd4RA.99

1. Ask your church for a list of widows and pick a few and visit them every other month. Find out what they like (food, favorite color, when their birthday is) and bring something once in a while. Talk to them; ask them how their day is going, and if they need anything special.
2. Expect to be there awhile (around an hour). They are lonely and need others to fellowship with. They may show you things they have made or gotten that are interesting to them. Listen and enjoy the time.

3. Depending on the time of the year you may want to do something special for them. For example, around Christmas time, get a few families or kids together and make some cookies and go caroling at their door. Because I am a singer in a choir at my church, that would be something that I would love to see at that time of year.
4. When you find out when their birthday is send them a card with a kind note inside, reminding them that you are thinking of them.
5. Pray for their needs before you leave. Focus on the needs they told you about and give them a big hug.

CHAPTER THREE

Hear me when I call, O God of my righteousness: thou hast enlarged me *when I was* in distress; have mercy upon me, and hear my prayer.

(Psalm 4:1)

Phone Calls

This section is for people who do not like to or cannot make house visits. It really is the same as making a house call except it is done over the phone. Usually a caregiver or lady from a Bible class or deacon's wife does this.

You're asking them the same question.

1. Ask when their birthday is so you can send them a card.
2. How their day is going and do they need anything you can pray about.
3. Do they need anything- a ride to church, a food run, or a ride to the doctor?
4. Ask how the kids are doing or pet if they have one.
5. Ask them if you can do a little devotional and pray with them today.

Here are 10 things that you should not say to a Widow:

1) "How are you doing?" (In a slow, low, monotone tone)

What people think they are saying: I am expressing concern and love.
What it sounds and feels like to a new widow: Seriously, is that a question? Do you really want that answered? Would you like to pull up a chair or maybe a sleeping bag? I'm a widow, a widow with a brain injury. I'm facing a whole new world. My

children have no father. I wake up every morning alone.

2) "At least you're young…"

What people think they are saying: You can go on and get remarried and live a happy life.
What it sounds and feels like to a new widow: At least I'm young? Hmmm. Wow. I'm pretty sure that being young does not make this any easier. I was going to spend the rest of my life with this person and being young enough to be able to spend it with someone else is of no comfort at all.
(I am a widow of 24 years and still have not found another life partner to fill that void)

3) "We have to understand grief does not have words - only tears."

Expect them to break down in tears when you least expect it - at the sound of the doorbell, at the sound of the telephone, at the sight of a couple walking hand in hand. All too soon the reality of being without him sets in and it will take time for them to let go of the past, but they will.

4) "It feels like an eternal winter. Everything is frozen and nothing comes alive."

They miss everything that they did with their life partner. It is very hard for them to make choices for the future. They feel like their life has ended as they know it, and may need help just getting out the door.

5) "Life never goes back to the way it was before your beloved died. Try as hard as you can, but everything has changed."

They have to find a reason to do things with others in their life, family, church, and work. We need to help them, but not push too hard. It has to be when they are ready. They have to be reminded that they will make mistakes and always ask for counsel in every part of their life.

6) "Grief does damage."

This doesn't mean that healing can't take place, but it takes time. Some widows don't want to talk to anyone those first couple of months. They ask, "Why me? It could have been somebody else. Sometimes they're even mad at God and the world for taking their life partner away. Sometimes we need to be sensitive and ask if they are ready for visitors.

7) "No one's going to get it."

Your biggest resource for understanding will be fellow widows, and even that person's grief journey is a different path. No one can and truly understands 100% how they feel. Remember that friends and family love them and want to help, even if they don't "get it."

8) "Find some good jokes; laughter is really good medicine."

Surround them with people who embrace laughter and find the humor in life. It's probably a safe bet that laughter is one thing that pulled me through some of the darkest of times. If I hadn't chosen to find the funny side of things, I don't know if I would have made it through.

9) " I am sorry for your loss."

What people think they are saying: I am expressing concern and Jove.
What it sounds and feels like to a new widow:
"If there is a "loss?" This makes them wonder where it is found? For the new widow, there is no found.

10) "Other widows will save their sanity."

> *When they feel it is the right time, they will want to know other people "more like them."*
> *The American Widow Project, TAPS, and numerous Facebook groups are great places to start, but the most important one is at your church. The big part of my current sanity is to these ladies who shared their experiences and feelings with me. However, all the widows I know are grateful for widows helping widows regardless of how far along they were when they met them.*

What I am getting at here is that you need to pick a widow and encourage her over the phone to get out of the house and do things and go to church. Those four walls come falling in after a while. They just need to hear a friendly voice to put a smile on their face.

HERE ARE SOME ENCOURAGING DEVOTIONAL PRAYERS OR POEMS THAT YOU MAY WANT TO USE:

COME TO ME, and rest in My Presence. I am constantly *thinking about you,* and I want you to become increasingly mindful of Me. Awareness of My Presence can *give you rest* even when you are quite busy. An inner peacefulness flows out of knowing *I am with you always.* This knowledge of

Me permeates your heart, mind, and spirit — and it can fill you with deep joy.

Many of My followers are so focused on the problems they see and the predictions they hear that they lose their joy. It becomes buried under multiple layers of worry and fear. When you realize this has happened in your life, bring all your concerns to Me. Talk with Me about each one, seeking My help and guidance. Ask Me to remove the anxious layers that have buried your joy. As you entrust your concerns into My care and keeping, your joy will begin to emerge again. Nurture this gladness by speaking or singing praises to *Me — the King of Glory* who loves you eternally. **(Sept 21 from Jesus Always Devotions by Sarah Young)**

Be Anxious About Nothing

Be anxious about nothing,
Let your spirit find great peace
In the assurance that God
Shall forever, always keep
A vigil watch over you,
And take care of all the needs
Of your heart most completely,
No matter what they might be.
And even though there are some
Things you cannot understand,
Be anxious about nothing,
Because you're safe in God's hands.

Steven Michael Schumacher

The poem is from **(Romans 15:13)**
Now the God of hope fills you with all joy and peace in believing, that ye may abound in hope through the power of the Holy Ghost.

Valley Of Indecision

The valley of indecision can oftentimes frightening be
—The choices that we make in life with outcome we
can't see; there's prayer and hope for God's Will only
>But waning faith can leave one lonely.
>As in this valley man's heart is tried
>Which way to choose and can't decide,
>For one path seems to be the right,
>The other path seems filled with light.
>And yet another with fields of green
>Is but a mirage when truth is seen.
>So know that God is there each stride
>Lovingly walking by our side.
>Speaking softly with words of calm,
>Just take His hand the journey long;
>He promised comfort without end,
>Would wait for us around each bend.
>One step with Him and then another,
>Each step leading onward, upward,
>Each step bringing hope renewed,
>For God is walking there with you.

Lynda Bryan Davis

Few reminders from God:
Matthew 11:28, Psalm 139:17, Matthew 28:20, Psalm 24:7

Here are a few of the books I have and use in my life:

A Daily Word 366 - *Scriptural Devotions for Growing Christians by Paul Chappell*

Rooted in Christ 366- - *Scriptural Devotions for Growing Christians by Paul Chappell*

A Word To The Wise - *Practical Advice from the Book of Proverbs by Paul Chappell*

RENEW- *90 Days of Spiritual Refreshment by Paul Chappell*

Jesus Always-365 *Devotions Embracing Joy in His Presence by Sarah Young*

Threads of Life, Fill My Heart with Joy, Pathway to Your Heart - *from the Salesian Collection — poetry and original artwork in our inspirational book series.*

I gave you a few, so find some of your own and share them. It's about giving the widow hope and joy from God's Word.

CHAPTER FOUR

And oppress not the widow, nor the fatherless, the stranger, nor the poor; and let none of you imagine evil against his brother in your heart.

(Zechariah 7:10)

Grief Counseling

I know when I was first a widow I was hurting a lot. And others widows are probably wondering when that hurt and pain are going to go away.

So How Do You Stop the Hurt? It took me time and a lot of prayer. I have to accept God's plan for my life and His will even if it does not feel good. I cannot continue to seek ways for the hurt to go away. I must seek for the best way to work with my hurt and carry on.

Three times the apostle Paul asked God to remove his "thorn in the flesh," yet God chose not to.

"For this thing I besought the Lord thrice, that it might depart from me.

And he said unto me, My grace is sufficient for thee: for my strength is made perfect in weakness. Most gladly therefore will I rather glory in my infirmities, that the power of Christ may rest upon me.

Therefore I take pleasure in infirmities, in reproaches, in necessities, in persecutions, in distresses for Christ's sake: for when I am weak, then am I strong."

(2 Cor. 12:8-10)

Regardless of the grace, Paul still had the weakness, the infirmity ... the hurt. Just as God did not remove Paul's hurt, He will not take mine or yours away. Since this is true, how do I take the hurt away? I can't, but by God's grace, in time the hurt will lessen for us, and we won't cry nearly as much. My goal is not to stop the hurt, but to access the grace (the power to accomplish God's will) that is already there for me!

My Goal

I can go through life
And never fear,
Because I know, my Lord,
You're forever near.
Whatever road I choose to roam,
Your love will always
Guide me home.
I yield myself and all I do,
And depend, my Lord, on You.
There's a peace that
Floods my soul
As I reach for You,
My God, my goal.
My goal is
With You by my side,
And forever more
With You abide.

Dona M. Maroney

My challenge to you is to lean on the grace given to you for your loneliness and to continue doing right in your circumstances. Be like the apostle Paul and glory in your infirmity that the power of Christ may rest upon you. It is true: we can't stop our hearts from hurting, and loneliness is something that is very real.

Moreover, God's grace was enough for Paul, and it should be completely sufficient for me…and for you!

Joy Is a State of Mind

Some say, "joy comes in the morning"
And often that is true,
But joy becomes a state of mind
When it abides in you.
Then it becomes a way of life,
The highlight of each day,
When your attitude is positive
Whatever comes your way.
When you put your faith in action,
You can smile through the tears
Because faith and joy are stronger
Than daily doubts and fears.
Joy spreads like ripples in a stream
Inspiring all who see,
For so many now are hurting
In our society.
Joy brings peace and contentment
And pleasant dreams at night
As stress levels are lowered
And our worries take flight.
A joy-filled heart beats smoother than
Hearts paralyzed by fear
And it becomes a state of mind
With nothing to fear.

Clay Harrison
These poems are found in **Fill My Heart With Joy**
from the Salesian Collection

This is something that was given to me in my Bible Group at church and I hope it encourages and helps you in your daily walk with the Lord as it does for me.

Here are a few things that a grief class at a church may offer you:

1) Counsel through the hard times:

Trouble is something that comes to every one of us at one time or another. As with
many things in life it is not a question of "if trouble will come" but "when trouble will
come." Hard times can be quite difficult. There is no one who will go through this life
without some pain and yes even grief. The big question is where we will go to get help,
relief, and a little understanding? In the middle of it all we may even have some big
questions for God. Does God really care about me? If God is good, then why is this happening to me?

2) How to respond to trouble and grief:

A few weeks of classes can help you take a good look at how to respond to trouble and grief in your life. You will learn how to respond to the suffering that can accompany trouble. The lessons that you will learn from the Word of God will help you to renew the hope that we should have in God and His plan for us. When this fallen world falls on us and it will, God wants us to have hope and trust in Him. You will walk along with others in this class who are hurting. They will encourage you to ask God to help you to be strengthened and equipped. In time, you will be able to someday help others who are hurting. As Paul came alongside of those who were hurting, we, too, wish to come alongside of you in your time of hurt. They promise to give you three things in this class:

1) the Word of God,
2) our caring heart,
3) a loving church family.

May we continue to grow in our faith that we are able to fully trust in a God who truly loves us when trouble and suffering enter our door.

CHAPTER FIVE

The blessing of him that was ready to perish came upon me: and I caused the widow's heart to sing for joy.

(Job 29:13)

Widows Support Groups

Here is a Grieving Widows Support Group I located on the internet:

Support Groups for widows - Heartache to healing: www.heartachetohealing.com/support-groups-for widows.

I still feel that your church is always going to be the best place to go when you lose someone as special as a loved one.

In what ways do churches help when you're grieving?

What could they do better?

Many churches help widows in many significant ways:
- Prayer: Congregational prayer for them on Sunday mornings, with their families and then in their home, in small group meetings, consistent, fervent prayer from the leadership of their church and from people in the congregation.
- Consistent Contact: Email, phone calls, cards, visits - we knew we were not alone in the struggle against loneliness.
- Meals and other offers of practical help.
- The support of other widows after my husband's death. They were my beacon in the darkness, showing me how to go on.
- The funeral service at the church and the reception after the graveside service: I felt so surrounded by the strength and love of my brothers and sisters in Christ.

I honestly cannot think of anything they could have done better. They were a model of how to do it right.

All It Takes Is a Smile

A smile is a happiness gift,
A lost and lonely heart it can lift;
So why not make someone's life worthwhile,
All it takes is a smile.

A smile is a bridge to the heart,
Joy it will bring you right from the start;
Your day will be happier all the while,
All it takes is a smile.

You can give this life-giving gift,
Whenever someone's soul is adrift;
Smiles will never go out of style,
Yes, all it takes is a smile.

Nora M. Bozeman

Just a reminder from God:
Only fear the LORD, and serve him in truth with all your heart: for consider how great things he hath done for you.

I Samuel 12:24
What do we do for the widow after the funeral service?
Here are a few ideas for a Widows Ministry at your church:

Widow's Ministry Purpose:

The purpose of a Widows Ministry is to provide a secure and honored sisterhood community for our widows to pursue their called ministries. This includes their encouragement by promoting and recognizing their many contributions to their church vision throughout the church body.

We should strive to help each widow to maintain her joy of life through committed personal ministers' readiness to "be there" and lovingly help them address existing or potential physical, mental, or spiritual "distress" speed bumps or barriers.

Personal Couples Ministry (PCM):

Widow's feedback can give high preference for a husband/wife team as their "up close and personal" ministers. A majority of PCMs are deacon couples but not a criterion.

Their goal is that each widow will have a PCM assigned to her. Some couples have more than one widow, but this is not always practical for everyone. Compatibility is sought for each PCM based on all parties' capabilities and needs which can change over time.

More PCM's are always needed. I do realize that some churches may have between 75 to over 200.

Handyman Ministry:

Everyone runs into situations where things don't work right. These are men who are skilled in a variety of auto, household, and property repairs, and are EAGER to use their skills to help widows. We know there are many widows who have help in these areas.

However, we also know there are widows who could really use handyman help but are reluctant to ask or are unaware of these ready services. We want them to call the church office for friendly and capable help.

Encouragement Ministry:

It is important that each widow is timely reminded that her church, and especially a dedicated group of ministers, have a special bond of love for them and are committed to honoring them with service. Social gatherings and encouragement cards should be used throughout the year so all widows will be so reminded.

Some social gatherings events could be around February, May, November, and December — at least four times a year.

Some Social gatherings ideas for events could be:

February: Sweetheart Day Dinner
May: Mother's Day Fellowship
November: Holiday Day Shopping Trip
December: Christmas Luncheon

Encouragement Cards: should be sent out once to three times a year.
Birthday month
Easter month
Christmas month

ORGANIZATIONS:

There should be a Deacon-led Widow Ministry Leadership Team (WMLT) or Director of a Widow's Ministry that provides the Ministry Plan, structure, and procedures for the Widow Ministry to function within the framework of the church. Ministers include pastors, staff, teachers, deacons and their wives, and numerous other adults with children, both singles and couples, all with a heart to minister to these special ladies who have so much to give.

CHAPTER SIX

And in those days, when the number of the disciples was multiplied, there arose a murmuring of the Grecians against the Hebrews, because their widows were neglected in the daily ministration.

(Acts 6:1)

Encouraging Books to Read

Do not get me wrong; we all need to read books any time of our life. But right now, that widow you are visiting or calling on the phone may need more help than you can give in a few visits a month. So here are some books that you may buy and give to help her on her path to recovery:

From One Widow to Another:

Conversations on the New You

"Widow" is one title women do not want to have. Yet, according to the Surgeon General's office, 800,000 people become widows or widowers every year in the United States alone. Every aspect of a widow's existence changes — like it or not, ready or not. These changes add to the emotional roller coaster that most women experience after losing their husband. Miriam Neff understands the ride. As she struggled to understand and accept her new role after her husband's death, she recognized the need for women to hear from others about their experiences and what helped them transition to this new stage of life. From One Widow to Another offers practical advice for those facing the loss of a spouse. Drawing from her own loss, Neff walks with the reader through practical issues to a sense of encouragement. By Miriam Neff

Getting to the Other Side of Grief:

Overcoming the Loss of a Spouse

Two healing professionals who both lost spouses to death provide empathy, valuable psychological insights, biblical observations, and male and female perspectives to help you experience grief in the healthiest, most complete way.

By Susan J. Zonnebelt- Smeengee and Robert C. De Vries

Letter to a Grieving Heart:

Comfort & Hope for Those Who Hurt

In this book, Billy Sprague offers the kind of compassion and insight that can only come from one who has lived through deep loss himself. Among other losses, he has had to face the death of a fiancee, a beloved grandmother, and a favorite college professor. From these experiences, he has drawn the kind of insight that will help others walk through the dark, seemingly endless times of grief. With honesty, passion, and perspective, he shares the little things that eased him forward and the words of comfort that carried him to a place of strength. Illustrated with restful, hope-filled photographs of nature, this is the ideal gift of comfort for anyone who is grieving a loss in their life. By Billy Sprague

Signs of Life: A Memoir

Twenty-four-year-old Natalie Taylor was leading a charmed life. At the age of twenty-four, she had a fulfilling job as a high school English teacher, a wonderful husband, a new house, and a baby on the way. Then, while visiting her sister, she gets the news that Josh has died in a freak accident. Four months before the birth of her son, Natalie is leveled by loss. What follows is an incredibly powerful emotional journey, as Natalie calls upon resources she didn't even know she had in order to re-imagine and re-build a life for her and her son. In vivid and immediate detail, Natalie documents her life from the day of Josh's death through the birth their son, Kai, as she struggles in her role as a new mother where everyone is watching her for signs of impending collapse. With honesty, raw pain, and most surprising, a wicked sense of humor, Natalie recounts the agonies and unexpected joys of her new life. By Natalie Taylor

Hope Heals:

Hope Heals is a keepsake journal created for teenagers and adults who have lost a loved one. This journal was created out of an appreciation and understanding of how difficult and life changing it is to experience the death of a loved one. The book serves as a tool to discover growth and strength in the midst of the pain. Elements of the book were first used in group and individual grief counseling sessions as part of Park Nicollet Foundation's Growing Through Grief program. This book provides a place to write details of a loved one's death and memories of their life, along with thoughts and feelings that are part of the healing process. By Sarah Kroenke

Daily Devotions

Everyday Comfort Meditations for Seasons of Grief People who are mourning the loss of a dear friend or beloved family member often feel alone, abandoned, and helpless. And those who want to comfort them can feel inadequate and at a loss for words. In Everyday Comfort, grievers will find thirty daily devotions to help them through their heartache. Respecting the griever's anguish and emotional turmoil, these devotions avoid platitudes and offer genuine empathy and wisdom. Subjects like recovery, facing death, normal grief and abnormal grief, and using the Psalms daily will help those who grieve examine the path through despair and take the next steps toward living life again. By Randy Becton

Something that you may want to read to a widow during a visit or over a phone call to encourage her:

It's God's Way

Sometimes I think I'm all alone
And it seems that no one cares.
When the specter of loneliness shadows me,
I wonder, does God hear my prayers?

It is then I seek out a garden,
Where flowers profusely bloom.
It is there I see the handwork of God ...
In a rose, in a tree, in the blossoms' perfume.

It is there God sends the bluebird
To sing its songs for me;
And the butterfly, too, plays its part...
It's God's way - it just has to be.

When a daisy lifts its happy face
To bid me a welcome "hello,"
It is then, and there, my loneliness is gone...
It's God's way-I just know!
In a garden, I know, I am never alone,
It is there I know God's love and grace.
It is there He wraps me in His loving arms
And gathers my loneliness in His embrace.

Charles Clevernger

Just a few reminders from God:
Learn to do well; seek judgment, relieve the oppressed, judge the fatherless, plead for the widow.

(Isaiah 1:17)

Sing to him, sing psalms unto him, talk ye of all his wondrous works.

(1 Chronicles 16:9)

Unto thee, O my strength, will I sing: for God is my defence, and the God of my mercy

(Psalm 59:17)

CHAPTER SEVEN

There is a conspiracy of her prophets in the midst thereof, like a roaring lion ravening the prey; they have devoured souls; they have taken the treasure and precious things; they have made her many widows in the midst thereof.

(Ezekiel 22:25)

Websites to Checkout

I do understand that some widows may not have a computer at home but you may be able help them by accessing some of these websites to get some of the questions answered that they may have.

Widow Net
www.widownet.org

Established in 1995, it is the first online information and self-help resource for, and by, widows and widowers.

Topics covered include grief, bereavement, recovery, and other information helpful to people of all ages, religious backgrounds, and sexual orientations, who have suffered the death of a spouse or life partner.

The Sisterhood of Widows-Widows Resources Site & Online
www.sisterhoodofwidows.com

An online community for widows and grievers, this website gives detailed support and strength for a widows health: physically, mentally, and spiritually.

Homepage - Hope for Widows
www.hopeforwidows.org

The foundation of Hope for Widows is firmly embedded in the bedrock of experience. From its leaders to its newest member, Hope for Widows is a support system for, and developed by, widowed women. Our vision is to create a strong network of widows. We seek to empower our members through shared experience. We open the door to a new world for widows, ensuring they do not go through their experience alone, but with life-long connections and lasting support.

These websites are for widows whom you cannot get through to yourself. A lot of widows just need to talk about their loss at the beginning. A lot of crying and wishing it were them that were gone and not their lost one.

A Quiet Place

Calmness and peace has entered my soul
As I rest in my secret place.
I open my mind and heart there within
As I come before Him in His grace.
Relaxing my mind, He enfolds me as I
Await His refreshment, in love.
My thoughts never wander, my breath's never quick, For I bask in the warmth from above.
And so, as I daily retreat to this space
Where at once I find calmness and peace.
All troubles and worries, all strife and concerns,
I lay there at our Master's feet.
He gathers them all and tucks them away;
No longer they're mine, but now His.
I leave my calm place and go back to the world,
Knowing all sins He forgives.
The next day I come to His firm embrace.
Once more I am home with Trinity Three
As I rest and relax in His space.

Ruthmarie Brooks Sliver

We are a non-denominational organization looking to assist widowed women, married or unmarried, who have lost their partner and are looking to find hope for a brighter day.

Just a few reminders from God:

And he arose, and rebuked the wind, and said unto the sea, "Peace, be still." And the wind ceased, and there was great calm.

(Mark 4:39)

The Lord says that we have to be careful how we take care of our widows. That we should give them all the help we can to make their lives joyful and needed in the world.

3   Thus saith the LORD; Execute ye judgment and righteousness, and deliver the spoiled out of the hand of the oppressor: and do no wrong, do no violence to the stranger, the fatherless, nor the widow, neither shed innocent blood in this place.

4   For if ye do this thing indeed, then shall there enter in by the gates of this house kings sitting upon the throne of David, riding in chariots and on horses, he, and his servants, and his people.

5   But if ye will not hear these words, I swear by myself, saith the LORD, that this house shall become a desolation.

(Jeremiah 22:3-5)

CHAPTER EIGHT

Thou hast sent widows away empty, and the arms of the fatherless have been broken.

(Job 22:9)

Financial Help

Here are a few poems that you can read or give to a widow to remind her that God is still there even through this loss.

Through It All

Through every heartache and trial,
God will meet our need.
It matters not our worldly wealth;
Faith is ours to believe.

Someday may never seem to end,
When each minute is like an hour.
God often brings us to our knees
Before restoring to us His power.

However old we may get to be,
There's always a lesson to learn.
We may not like what's in His plan;
But at its end, for Him we yearn.

God is in the rescue business
When our arms are too short to reach.
He saves from what we deserve
And gives eternal life to each.

M. Elaine Fowser

To Face Each Day

When life gets hard, and oh, so dreary,
As you struggle through each day,
Your faith seems weak and try as you might,
You just cannot seem to pray.
He knows your struggles,
He feels your pain;
He's right there at your side,
Receive His help, drink in His love.
In Him may you always abide.

Mary Ann Jameson

Just a few reminders from God:

Examine me. O LORD, and prove me; try my reins and my heart. **(Psalm 26:2)**

(For we walk by faith, not by sight)

(2 Corinthians 5:7)

Here are a few books to help new widows get through financial changes because of the lost husband. You can suggest these books if your widow has questions and problems handling any of these issues.

Moving Forward on Your Own: A Financial Guidebook for Widows

A husband's death is possibly the most devastating event a woman will experience. She might wonder if she will be able to make it on her own. She may feel overwhelmed and not know what to do next without her partner. Kathleen's guidebook helps widows be more confident, knowledgeable, and secure about their money matters. The book integrates basic financial information with self-reflective exercises that encourage financial self-assurance. Kathleen is honest about her own struggles as a widow, and she holds empathy for others. This unique guidebook is presented in a beautiful format, to help heal a woman's soul as well as gently focus on money matters. The book is not intended to teach women everything about money and financial planning immediately. When someone is emotionally overwhelmed, it's not wise to overload one's focus. Rather, widows are invited to begin looking at their money issues and then take actions in a way that builds confidence ... as they transition into a new financial life on their own. This book may be used independently, in a collaborative approach with a professional, or in a group with facilitated conversation (such as a widow's support group, congregation class, or a women's community gathering). It's also an appropriate gift book for a widowed friend or family member.

By Kathleen M. Rehl Ph.D CFP

The Widow's Financial Survival Guide

For recently widowed women, times are hard enough without having to worry about money. Unfortunately, many women are left in financial chaos after a spouse's death and become vulnerable to costly mistakes and even outright scams. With this in mind, one of today's foremost financial experts has put together a step-by-step guide specifically for widows. Thorough and accessible, it addresses a wide range of legal and financial issues, including estates * taxes * IRAs and 401(k)s * government benefits* business* budgeting * re-marriage * investments * scams and frauds* housing and more.

By Nancy Dunnan

CHAPTER NINE

And she was a widow of about fourscore and four years, which departed not from the temple, but served God with fastings and prayers night and day.

(Luke 2:37)

Church Help

Here are four steps that we can take to minister to widows at our churches:

1) Educate our congregation to prepare for the eventuality of death.
a) A widow's most difficult problem is that of working through her grief.
b) Financial management of the family, home, a business, an estate, and investments.
c) She crash-lands into an unfamiliar world of difficult decisions.

2) Encourage a widow to join a widow's helping-widows group.
a) No one can help a widow as effectively as another widow.
b) If you do not have a widows group, start one up.
c) Have a list of helpful books on widowhood in your church library.

3) Follow the lead of the early church and designate a deacon or director of a widow's ministry to look after the needs of each widow.
a) *Thayer's Greek-English Lexicon* gives the Hebraistic meaning of the word *episkeptomai*, translated "visit," as "to look upon in order to help or benefit, to look after, to have a care for, and provide for."
b) Just to make a social call will not fulfill James' injunction. So if a deacon or layman is appointed to visit a widow in his charge at least once a month over a period of, say, two years, this is what it means:

1) When he makes his call and finds the bathroom faucet dripping, he fixes it.
2) If the lawn needs mowing and there are no able-bodied children in the family to do it, he mows it.
3) If the roof leaks, he repairs it.
4) If the house needs painting and she cannot afford to have it done, he will recruit others in the fellowship to do the job, so she will be proud of her home.
5) If she needs counsel in business and financial matters, and he does not feel qualified in this area, he will recommend the right person.

4) Provide each widow with:

a) Names, addresses, and telephone numbers of the persons and agencies in the community to whom she can go for help.

b) Pastor or deacon should list realtors, bankers, social workers, counselors, and a mechanic who won't overcharge for auto repairs, and so on.

If anyone reaching out to help a widow who needs help in any of these areas, he should reach out to the fellowship in the church to do the job.

Unwrap the Day Before You

Unwrap the day before you
As if it were a gift
That's sent to you from Heaven
To give your soul a lift.
Each day contains a blessing
That was gift-wrapped above
And delivered by God's angels
With messages of love.
Every day is far too precious
To be squandered away,
For it withers like Autumn leaves
And "nothing gold can stay."
Unwrap the day and savor,
The moments one by one,
And it surely will amaze you
How much you can get done.
Seize every precious moment
Before it fades away,
For some are answers to the prayers
You asked for yesterday.
For some, this will be the last
Sunrise they'll ever see.
Unwrap the day before you,
Give thanks and let it be.

Clay Harrison

Just a reminder from God:

Because he hath set his love upon me, therefore will I deliver him: I will set him on high, because he hath known my name.

(Psalm 91:14)

Help from your church is not just for widows. Here are few things that most churches do:

Food or meals
Pay hospital or normal house bills
Repairs on houses
Cutting the lawn
A safe place to volunteer

These are things that a lot of churches do for their faithful church members. Maybe we should do more.

CONCLUSION

As we have seen, our helping widows can be of value to others and ourselves. With that in mind, let's take a look at a few ways that an understanding of God's reasons for helping widows might lead us to the right response.

First, Chapter One, "Prayer," we learned how to grieve healthily by using John 11:32-37.
That when we pray for others, we are helping them gain strength to get through the day. Prayer is influential to our lives and others' lives. When we are praying, God is working.

Second, In Chapter Two, "Visits," expect to be there awhile (around an hour); they are lonely and need others to fellowship with.

They may show you things they have made or gotten that are interesting to them. Listen and enjoy the time.

Third, in Chapter Three, "Phone Calls," there are 10 things that you should not say to a Widow. "Grief does damage." *Some time we need to be sensitive; ask if they are ready for visitors.*

Fourth, in Chapter Four, "Grieving Classes," in grieving classes, there is counsel through the hard times and there is help as you learn how to respond to trouble and grief.

Fifth, in Chapter Five, "Widows Support Groups," our church will always be the best place to go for support. That we can do more for our widows.

Sixth, in Chapter Six, "Encouraging Books to Read," those books can give widows hope for healing. Books also let the widow see that there are others out there hurting just like them. When we read the Bible, it shows us that we need to plead for the widow and encourage them through this time in their life.

Seventh, in Chapter Seven, "Websites to Checkout," we have found out that there are many websites out there with helpful topics covered including grief, bereavement, recovery, and other information helpful to people of all ages, religious backgrounds, and sexual orientations who have suffered the death of a spouse or life partner. Please make sure to check with your churches before using.

Eighth, in Chapter Eight," Financial Help," some of these books helps and addresses a wide range of legal and financial issues, including estates * taxes * IRAs and 401(k)s * government benefits* business* budgeting * re-marriage * investments * scams and frauds * housing and more. Check with your church; some do have financial departments that can help the widow in need.

Ninth, in Chapter Nine," Church Help," we need to be educating our congregation to prepare for the eventuality of death. We have learned that our church is great at helping widows, but they still need to do more.

Just a last devotion from God and Sarah Young

LET MY UNFAILING LOVE *be your comfort;* "Comfort" eases grief and trouble; it also gives strength and hope. The best source of these blessings is My constant Love that will never, ever fail you. No matter what is happening in your life, this Love can console you and cheer you up. However, you must make the effort to turn to Me for help. I am always accessible to you, and I delight in giving you everything you need.

I have complete, perfect understanding of you and your circumstances. My grasp of your situation is far better than yours. So beware of being overly introspective —-trying to figure things out by looking inward, leaving Me out of the equation. When you realize you have done this, turn to Me with a brief prayer: "Help me, Jesus." Remind yourself that I am the most important part of the equation of your life! Relax with Me awhile, letting My loving Presence comfort you. In the world you will have trouble; but be a good cheer, I have overcome the world. **(October 25, from Jesus Always Devotions by Sarah Young)**

Just a few reminders from God:

Let, I pray thee, thy merciful kindness be for my comfort, according to thy word unto thy servant

Psalm 119:76

The LORD will give strength unto his people; the LORD will bless his people with peace.

Psalm 29:11

Why art thou cast down, O my soul? and *why* art thou disquieted in me? hope thou in God: for I shall yet praise him *for* the help of his countenance.

Psalm 42:5

These things I have spoken unto you, that in me ye might have peace. In the world ye shall have tribulation: but be of good cheer; I have overcome the world.

John 16:33

Every time I start a book, I pray for God to give me a poem or song to go along with them. This time I received one from a friend who is a widow.

JAMIE PULOS-FRY

A Widow's Tears

We are special in the eyes of God,
 held by His Almighty hand.
Crying in secret, sorrowful hearts,
 trying our best to stand.
No one to talk with, to share our day,
 quiet silence along the way.
We want to live by faith, not by sight,
 loneliness fills our night.
God guides every step with His love and grace.
 Surrounding us in our special place,
we are widows by name and in our heart.
 Trusting in God and singing.
 How Great Thou Art.

Nancy Lusk

I hope this helps you understand more of what widows go through on a daily basis.

INDEX OF SCRIPTURES

I Samuel
12:24 40

I Chronicles
16:9 50

Job
22:9 55
29:13 38

Psalm
4:1 23
26:2 57
29:11 68
42:5 68
59:17 50
91:14 64
119:76 68

Back Isaiah
1:17 49

Jeremiah
22:3-5 54

Ezekiel
22:25 51

Zechariah
7:10 32

Luke
2:37 60

John
11:32-37 12
16:33 68

Acts
6:1 44

Romans
15:13 30

II Corinthians
5:7 57

Galatians
6:2 12

Hebrews
13:5 18

James
1:27 20

I Timothy
2:1-4 13
5:3 11

REFERENCE BOOKS

Jackson, Joanna. <u>The Abundant Single Life</u>.
Tennessee: Sword of The Lord. 2012.

Salesian Missions. <u>Threads of Life from the Salesian Collection</u>
New York: Salesian Missions. 2013. Volumes 58

Salesian Missions. <u>Fill My Heart With Joy from the Salesian Collection</u>
New York: Salesian Missions 2015. Volumes 63

Salesian Missions. <u>Pathway to Your Heart from the Salesian Collection</u>
New York: Salesian Missions 2014. Volumes 60

Word Ministries, Inc. <u>Prayers That Avail Much Volumes 1& 2</u>
Georgia: Harrison House, Inc.1989

Young, Sarah. <u>Jesus Always.</u>
Tennessee:Thomas Nelson. 2016

ABOUT THE AUTHOR

Jamie Pulos-Fry

Is a faithful member of Lancaster Baptist Church, Lancaster, California. She likes to serve and volunteer in various areas of the church. This is her third book, and she hopes it will be a great help in future widow ministry choices in your life.

For additional books by
Jamie Pulos-Fry visit
www.blurb.com

TWO 4 AVALON PUBLICATIONS

This book is about helping others in the future with the same trials that you have been through. You have overcome something early in life and can encourage others what you have learned and can pass on to others will not quitting on yourself or others.
(68 pages, Paperback)

This book is about being the best volunteer that God would like you to be, by being faithful, being a servant and helping others will serving at church or any place that you which to help others.
(50 pages, Paperback)

www.ingramcontent.com/pod-product-compliance
Lightning Source LLC
LaVergne TN
LVHW020415070526
838199LV00054B/3621